Sponges
and Other Minor Phyla

Sally Morgan

Raintree

Chicago, Illinois

For information, address the publisher:
Raintree, 100 N. LaSalle, Suite 1200, Chicago, IL 60602

Produced for Raintree by
White-Thomson Publishing Ltd.

Consultant: Dr. Rod Preston-Mafham
Page layout by Tim Mayer
Photo research by Morgan Interactive Ltd.

Originated by Dot Gradations Ltd.
Printed in China by WKT Company Limited

09 08 07 06 05
10 9 8 7 6 5 4 3 2 1

Library of Congress Cataloging-in-Publication Data
Morgan, Sally.
   Sponges and other minor phyla / Sally Morgan.
      p. cm. -- (Animal kingdom)
   Includes bibliographical references and index.
   ISBN 1-4109-1053-9 (lib. bdg. : hardcover) -- ISBN 1-4109-
1349-X (pbk.)
   1. Sponges--Juvenile literature. 2. Cnidaria--Juvenile literature.
3. Worms--Juvenile literature. 4. Echinodermata--Juvenile
literature. I. Title. II. Series: Animal kingdom (Chicago, Ill.)
   QL371.6.M67 2005
   593.4--dc22

                                    2004007606

Acknowledgments
The publisher would like to thank the following for permission
to reproduce copyright materials : Adds, John p. 30; Corbis pp.
6, 61; Digital Vision p. 57 bottom; Ecoscene **contents** main
image (John Liddiard), **contents** left and right (Jeff Collett), 4
(Phillip Colla), 5 left (John Liddiard), 8 (Jeff Collett), 9 top (John
Liddiard), 9 bottom (Phillip Colla), 11 bottom (Jeff Collett),
12 left, 13 (John Liddiard), 15 (Phillip Colla), 21 main (John
Liddiard), 23 bottom (Phillip Colla), 26 (Kjell Sandved), 29
bottom (John Lewis), 34 top (Wayne Lawler), 34 bottom (Kjell
Sandved), 35 (Mark Caney), 37 top (Kjell Sandved), 37 bottom
(Mark Caney), 39 right (Jeff Collett), 44 bottom (Phillip Colla),
46, 47 (John Liddiard), 48 (Jeff Collett), 49 bottom (John
Liddiard), 51 top (Kjell Sandved), 54 (John Liddiard), 55 top
(Mark Caney), 55 bottom (Martha Collard), 56 (John Liddiard),
57 top (Wayne Lawler), 60 top (Frank Blackburn), 60 bottom
(Jeff Collett); Ecoscene-Papilio pp. 18 main (Steve Jones), 28, 31
top, 33, 38-39, 40, 41 top (Robert Pickett), 52 top (Peter
Tatton), Mediscan p 31 bottom; Nature Photo Library pp. 7 top
(Jeff Rotman), 21 inset (David Shale), 27 bottom (Sinclair
Stammers), 36 (Constantinos Petrinos); NHPA pp. 5 right
(Trevor McDonald), 11 top (G Bernard), 12-13 (Image Quest
3-D), 14 top (M Walker), 14 bottom (Image Quest 3-D), 17 top
(Michael Patrick O'Neill), 17 bottom (Norbert Wu), 20 (Rich
Kirchner), 22 (Peter Parks), 23 top (Anthony Bannister), 24
(ANT), 25 (Image Quest 3-D), 27 top, 29 top (M Walker), 32
top (Image Quest 3-D), 38 left (B Jones and M Shimlock), 41
bottom (Nigel Callow), 42 top (Stephen Dalton), 42 bottom
(Martin Harvey), 43 (Anthony Bannister), 45 (Trevor
McDonald), 49 top (Pete Atkinson), 50 (Trevor McDonald), 51
bottom (G Bernard), 52 bottom, 53 (B Jones and M Shimlock);
Photodisc **title**, pp. 10, 16, 19, 44 top, 57 bottom, 58, 59, 62,
63, 64; Premaphoto Wildlife pp. 7 bottom (Cliff Nelson), 32
bottom (Preston Mafham).

Front cover image of sponges colonizing a shipwreck is
reproduced with permission of Ecoscene (V & W); back cover
image of a sea star is reproduced with permission of Digital
Vision.

Every effort has been made to contact copyright holders of any
material reproduced in this book. Any omissions will be rectified
in subsequent printings if notice is given to the publisher.

Contents

Introducing Sponges and Other Minor Phyla

Sponges, cnidarians, worms, and echinoderms are all invertebrates. They are animals that do not have backbones. These groups of animals are found around the world. Earthworms live in soil, while sponges, cnidarians (jellyfish and corals), and echinoderms (sea stars and sea urchins) are found in coral reefs and shallow coastal waters.

Animals without backbones

Animals such as mammals, birds, and fish have backbones that support their bodies. Invertebrates do not have backbones, so they need some other form of support. The sea star gets its support from spiny plates that lie just beneath the skin. Many invertebrates, such as the earthworm, have a hydroskeleton. This means that their skeleton is formed from a fluid-filled body space. The fluid pushes against the body wall and makes it fairly rigid. A few invertebrates, such as jellyfish, have no skeletons. They are supported by the water in which they live.

▼ These anemones belong to the phylum Cnidaria. Their simple bodies do not have any skeletons.

Classification key	
KINGDOM	Animalia
PHYLA	Porifera, Cnidaria, Plathelminthes, Nematoda, Annelida, Echinodermata
SPECIES	20,000 (total for all these phyla)

Sponges, jellyfish, and many other invertebrates spend their entire lives in water. Most live in salt water, but a few are found in the freshwater of ponds, lakes, and rivers. Some invertebrates, such as the earthworm, live on land. Most invertebrates can move around. However, a surprising number cannot. They stay in the same place all the time and are called sessile. Others are described as sedentary because they move very little.

The groups of animals that are featured in this book are sponges, cnidarians, flatworms, roundworms, segmented worms, and echinoderms.

▲ These peacock worms are segmented worms that belong to the phylum Annelida.

▲ Sea stars are spiny-skinned invertebrates that belong to the phylum Echinodermata. They are closely related to sea urchins and brittle stars.

Classification

Living organisms are classified, or organized, according to how closely related one organism is to another. A species is a group of individuals that are similar to each other and that can interbreed with one another. For example, human beings belong to the species *Homo sapiens*. Species are grouped together into genera (singular: genus). A genus may contain a number of species that share some features. Genera are grouped together in families; families are grouped into orders; and orders are grouped into classes. Classes are grouped together in phyla (singular: phylum) and finally, phyla are grouped into kingdoms. Kingdoms are the largest groups. Sponges and all the other invertebrate animals belong to the animal kingdom.

Sponges

A sponge is the simplest of animals. Its body does not have any organs or nerves. It is simply a collection of cells held together by a network of fibers. Sponges do not move from one place to another. They are sessile animals, which means they stay attached to the same place. Most attach themselves to any suitable surface, such as rocks, seaweed, or even other animals. A few bore into rocks, shells, or coral.

Most sponges are marine. They are found in all of the seas, mainly in shallow water. However, a few are found in deep water. Sponges even occur in great numbers in the cold waters around Antarctica, where they can grow to large sizes. A few sponges live in freshwater.

Classification key

PHYLUM	Porifera
CLASSES	4 (Calcarea, Demospongiae, Hexactinellida, Sclerospongiae)
ORDERS	18
SPECIES	10,000

◀ Sponges come in an incredible variety of colors and shapes. These are tube sponges, which are open at one end and closed at the other. Other sponges are spheres, branching, or threadlike.

Skeleton and shape

The skeleton of the sponge has two main parts. There are fibers of collagen called spongin and rods with many points called spicules. Spicules may be made from silica or calcium carbonate. Spicules provide support as well as protection from predators. Few predators try to eat sponges—it would be like trying to swallow a mouthful of splinters!

Since sponges do not have a nervous system, they hardly react to the environment around them. The only reaction they show is to slowly change the size of the openings (osculums) through which water leaves their bodies. This is triggered by changes in the water around them, such as a change in the temperature or current. Sponges also lack coordination between cells for growth and, as a result, are of irregular size and shape. Often individual sponges are part of a larger mass, or colony, and it is almost impossible to identify individuals, other than by their osculums.

Protected by poisons

Sponges have few predators. Over millions of years, they have developed an array of poisons to keep away animals that might eat them and plants that might grow over them. These chemicals are so effective that scientists are trying to identify them for use in medicines.

Amazing facts

- A living bath sponge looks more like a piece of raw liver than the sponges we are used to using. The sponges are killed by boiling them. This leaves the skeleton behind. The skeleton is cleaned and trimmed for human use.
- Millions of years ago, some of the first reefs were made of sponges. The corals later outperformed them as reef-forming animals.

▲ Some sponges grow to a great size. The osculum of this sponge is large enough for a diver to swim inside.

▲ The azure vase sponge is one of the most attractive sponges. It has a light blue to purple color.

Feeding and Life Cycle

Sponges do not have mouths. Instead, they have tiny pores in their outer walls through which water is drawn. Cells in the walls filter particles of food from the water. The water enters a central cavity and is then expelled through the large opening called the osculum. The water flows in one direction and is driven by the beating of flagella—long, hairlike structures that line the surface of the cavity.

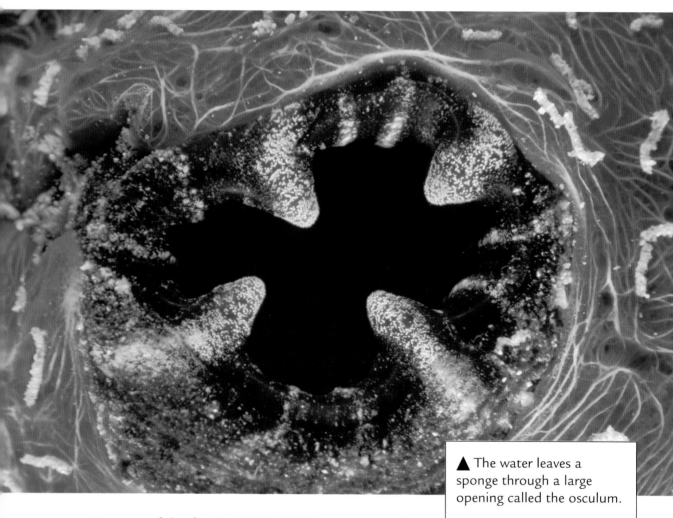

▲ The water leaves a sponge through a large opening called the osculum.

Sponges of the family Cladorhizidae are unusual in that they are carnivores. They feed by capturing and digesting animals such as small crustaceans. When the sponge comes into contact with its prey, its spicules stick to the prey so it cannot escape. The sponge's cells move around the prey and pour digestive juices over its body. Slowly the body of the prey is broken down. Then the sponge cells absorb the nutrients.

▲ Scientists are unsure why sponges come in so many colors. The vivid colors may be a warning that the sponge is poisonous or distasteful, or they may be a form of protection from harmful rays of sunlight.

Life cycle

Sponges reproduce by both asexual and sexual means. Asexual reproduction involves only one parent, and all the offspring are identical to the parent. Sponges that reproduce asexually produce buds. A bud consists of a collection of cells of various kinds inside a protective covering. The bud is released and it settles on the seabed and grows into a new sponge. All the new sponges are identical to the parent sponge that produced the bud.

Sexual reproduction involves two parents. Most sponges that undergo sexual reproduction are hermaphrodites. This means each sponge produces both eggs and sperm, but at different times of year. The sponges release sperm that are carried to other sponges to fertilize the eggs. A fertilized egg develops into a ciliated larva (a larva covered in tiny hairs called cilia). These larvae swim in the water and then settle on the seabed where they develop into young sponges.

Amazing facts

- Some of the smaller species of Demospongiae bore into mollusk shells, leaving the shell riddled with tiny holes.
- If a sponge is forced though a sieve, so that it is separated into individual cells, these cells will eventually reorganize themselves back into a sponge.
- Sometimes young prawns enter sponges and live inside them until they become too large to get out again.

▶ This close-up view of the gray moon sponge shows a number of osculums on the upper surface of the sponge.

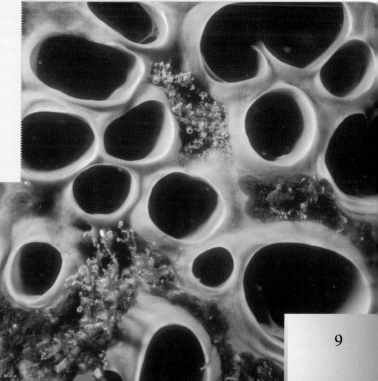

Sponge Classification

Sponges belong to the phylum Porifera. A single sponge species may occur in different shapes, so identification often depends on the type and shape of the spicules, which are unique to each species. In the past, the classification of sponges was based just on the types of spicules. This created four classes of sponges: Calcarea, Demospongiae, Hexactinellida, and Sclerospongiae. However, recent evidence taken from fossil sponges suggests that the Sclerospongiae are not sufficiently different to be classified separately from the other classes.

Calcarea

Calcarea sponges are the only class of sponges that have spicules made of calcium carbonate. The spicules have one, three, or four rays or points. There are approximately 100 species. Most calcarea sponges are small sponges found in shallow water, in caves, and on seaweed.

Demospongiae

Demospongiae make up the largest class of sponges with 9,500 species. It includes the best-known group of sponges: the bath sponges. These sponges are found in both shallow and deep water, nearly always on a solid surface. Demospongiae have spicules made from silica with one, two, or four rays. The sponges can reach more than 3 feet (1 meter) in length or width and are often brightly colored.

▲ The vase shape of this sponge does not help in its identification. Cells must be collected and examined under a microscope in order to identify the species.

Amazing facts

- So many sponges of the class Demospongiae are collected for use as bath sponges that some species are threatened with extinction.
- Some sponges found in freshwater are bright green. The color comes from single-celled algae living in cells of the sponges.

Hexactinellida

The Hexactinellida, or glass sponges, have spicules made from silica with 6 rays. There are about 500 species living in cold water at depths of between 650 and 6,500 feet (200 and 2,000 meters). One beautiful example is a sponge called Venus's flower basket. It has an intricate 3-dimensional skeleton that is only structurally possible because of the variety of ways in which the 6-rayed spicules fit together.

▲ The Venus' flower basket is named after its beautiful lacework of silica spicules. It is found in deep water off the Philippines.

Sclerospongiae

The coralline sponges, or Sclerospongiae, are an unusual class in which the sponges have a skeleton of silica and calcium carbonate. There is a thin living layer containing spicules of silica that covers a massive solid skeleton made of calcium carbonate. A few living species are found on coral reefs around the West Indies and in the Pacific Ocean.
The remaining species exist only as fossils.

Classification key

PHYLUM	Porifera
CLASSES	**4 (Calcarea, Demospongiae, Hexactinellida, Sclerospongiae)**
FAMILIES	80
SPECIES	10,000

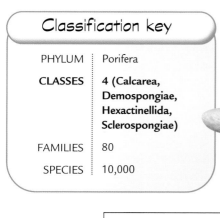

▶ Sponges come in a great range of shapes. One of the most unusual is this hand-shaped sponge.

Cnidaria

Sea anemones, corals, and jellyfish are all examples of cnidarians. These are sac-shaped animals with tentacles covered in sting cells.

Body shapes

Cnidarians do not have heads. They have a single body opening that is called the mouth. The body is saclike and encloses a large central cavity called the enteron that connects to the outside through the mouth. The enteron is used for digestion and for gas exchange, a process in which oxygen is taken in and carbon dioxide is given out. The mouth is surrounded by tentacles that are studded with sting cells. Most cnidarians are radially symmetrical. They have many lines of symmetry around a central point.

▶ Jellyfish have bell-shaped bodies and many long tentacles that hang in the water below their bells.

Classification key

PHYLUM	Cnidaria
CLASSES	Anthozoa, Scyphozoa, Hydrozoa, Cubozoa
ORDERS	7
SPECIES	approximately 9,000

▼ Soft corals are brightly colored and belong to the class Anthozoa.

The tentacles are arranged in a circle around the mouth and covered in sting cells.

The body of a cnidarian has two cell layers.

The slimy disc at the bottom allows the anemone to slide around very slowly and grip the rocks firmly.

▲ This dahlia anemone belongs to the class Anthozoa. Anemones grip the rocks so firmly that it is almost impossible to pull them off.

Two cell layers

Cnidarians are described as being diploblastic. This means that their bodies and tentacles consist of two cell layers: an inner layer called the endoderm and an outer layer called the ectoderm. Between the two cell layers is the mesogloea, which joins them together.

Feeding

All cnidarians are carnivorous. They use their tentacles and sting cells to capture their prey. There are several different kinds of sting cells. One type releases a thread that ends in a poisonous barb. The thread shoots out with such force that the barb pierces the body of the prey and then releases a poison that paralyzes the animal. The other types of sting cells release threads that hold the prey. Some stick to the prey while others wrap themselves around it. The sting cells are used only once and then have to be replaced.

Amazing facts

- The tiny box jellyfish is the size of a peanut and is probably the most poisonous animal on Earth. It is found in warm oceans around the world and is known to have killed people swimming in the water.
- Cnidarians can distinguish between food and inedible objects. A piece of paper that lands on a sea anemone would not trigger the sting cells.
- The thick layer of mesogloea in a jellyfish protects it from the buffeting of the sea.

Life Cycle

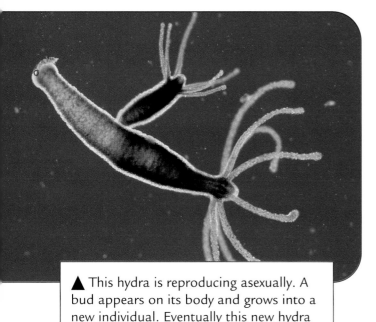

▲ This hydra is reproducing asexually. A bud appears on its body and grows into a new individual. Eventually this new hydra will break away.

Cnidarians have a complex life cycle. Most exist in two forms: the polyp and the medusa. The polyp is the sedentary form found on the seabed or on a coral reef. A typical polyp is a sea anemone that has a ring of tentacles around its mouth. The medusa looks completely different from the polyp. It has a bell-shaped body like a jellyfish. Most cnidarians exist as a polyp for part of their life and as a medusa for the rest. They alternate between polyp and medusa. However, there are some cnidarians, such as sea anemones and corals, that exist only as polyps.

Polyp and medusa

The cnidarian life cycle begins with the polyp. The polyp reproduces asexually to produce more identical polyps. This usually happens by budding. A bulge appears on the body wall of the polyp and develops into a new polyp. In some species, the bud grows, breaks off, and develops into a new individual. In others, the new individual remains attached. As more individuals form, a colony develops with all of the members of the colony connected by living tissue.

▶ This larval anemone, with its tiny tentacles, will settle on the seabed.

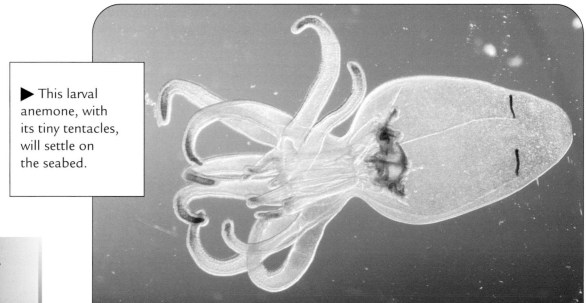

Amazing facts

- The word *polyp* came from the French word *poulpe*, which means "octopus," because an early French naturalist thought the tentacles of a cnidarian resembled the tentacles of the octopus.
- The medusa is named after the female figure, Medusa, from Greek mythology. She was loved by the god of the sea, and a jealous goddess turned her hair into snakes. The many tentacles on a cnidarian medusa reminded naturalists of Medusa's hair.

When conditions are right—such as at a particular time of year or when the water reaches the right temperature— the polyp produces a medusa that swims away. The medusa undergoes sexual reproduction. It produces eggs and sperm that are released into the sea. The sperm fertilize the eggs. Each fertilized egg develops into a larva, a pear-shaped animal covered in cilia. Then the larva undergoes a change in form, or metamorphosis. It settles on the seabed or rock, becomes attached, and grows into a polyp. The life cycle begins again.

Members of the class Anthozoa, such as sea anemones, are different from other cnidarians because they do not have a medusa stage. Some of their polyps can reproduce sexually by producing gametes, or sex cells. However, anthozoans rely on asexual reproduction to increase their numbers.

▶ Many tiny anemones can be seen under the tentacles of this adult anemone.

The Flower Animals

Members of the class Anthozoa are often called flower animals because of their bright colors and the way their tentacles form a ring like a flower's petals. They are marine animals and include corals, which build reefs in tropical waters, as well as sea anemones, sea fans, and sea pens. They are an ancient group of animals that date back at least 550 million years. Anthozoans are found in the intertidal zone along the coasts, in the shallow, warm waters around tropical islands, and even in the ocean trenches at depths of more than 3 miles (6 kilometers).

Anthozoan features

An anthozoan polyp has a cup-shaped body, with a mouth surrounded by a ring of hollow tentacles. Anthozoa range in size from less than 1 inch (2.5 centimeters) to more than 30 feet (10 meters) across. They have sting cells to catch prey, just like other cnidarians. Sea anemones can feed on surprisingly large prey, such as fish and crabs. The smaller anthozoans, such as corals, have algae in their cells that provide them with food. They use their sting cells as protection against predators such as snails, sea stars, and sea spiders.

◀ Some anemones, such as these strawberry anemones, are found grouped together. However, other anemone species are solitary animals.

▲ A sea pen looks somewhat like a feather. It has a central polyp with many lateral polyps arranged as side branches.

Reproduction

Anemones reproduce asexually by simply pulling apart into two halves. They can also reproduce sexually by producing gametes (eggs and sperm) that are released into the water. The resulting larvae settle on rocks and grow into new anemones.

Anthozoan classes

Anthozoans are divided into three subclasses. The Zoantharia includes the hard corals and most sea anemones. The Octocorallia includes the sea pens, soft corals, and sea fans. The third subclass, the Ceriantipatharia, includes the burrowing sea anemones and black corals.

▲ These sea anemones use their sting cells as weapons as they fight for position on the seabed.

Amazing facts

- Some sea anemones live on the shells of snails and crabs. They are carried around by their hosts. They may get food scraps from their hosts. The hosts are protected from predators by the anemones' stinging tentacles.

- Sea anemones fight over territory, using their sting cells against other anemones. They keep stinging until the other anemone moves away. Sometimes these fights result in an anemone's injury or death.

- There is a sea slug that actually eats sea anemones. Its stomach is lined with a protective coating to prevent injury from unexploded sting cells.

Classification key

PHYLUM	Cnidaria
CLASS	**Anthozoa**
SUBCLASSES	Zoantharia, Octocorallia, Ceriantipatharia
SPECIES	more than 6,500

Corals

Running down the length of the east coast of Australia is the Great Barrier Reef, a huge coral reef that can be seen from space. Amazingly, it was built by tiny animals called corals over thousands of years. Corals are cnidarians that are related to sea anemones.

Classification key

PHYLUM	Cnidaria
CLASS	Anthozoa
SUBCLASS	**Zoantharia, Octocorallia**
SPECIES	approximately 1,000

▶ At first sight, a coral reef looks like a garden, but corals are not plants. Coral reefs are colonies of thousands of tiny animals.

Hard and soft corals

There are two types of warm water corals: hard (or stony) corals and soft corals. Hard corals are responsible for building coral reefs. The hard corals live in colonies of individual polyps that share a common skeleton. The body of the polyp occupies a little cup that is attached at the bottom. The polyp secretes a skeleton made of calcium carbonate, or limestone. When the polyps die, they leave behind their skeletons. New polyps grow on top of the old ones, so over time the colony gets larger. The construction of a reef takes thousands—sometimes millions—of years.

▲ Soft corals have flexible skeletons made of a protein called gorgonin. Their skeletons also contain calcium carbonate, but only in clumps of spicules.

Feeding

Corals use their tentacles to capture zooplankton, the small animals that live in the water. Most corals extend their polyps and tentacles only at night when zooplankton is most abundant. However, the soft corals keep their polyps open throughout the day. The reef-building corals also get food from algae called zooxanthellae that live in their cells. The zooxanthellae carry out photosynthesis, using light and carbon dioxide to make carbohydrates. Some of these carbohydrates are given to the coral. The reef-building corals can live only in warm, shallow water down to depths of about 330 feet (100 meters) because their algae need light to photosynthesize. This extra supply of food allows them to grow quickly and to build new skeletons. The zooxanthellae also give the corals their color.

Reproduction

Coral polyps can reproduce asexually by dividing in half. They also reproduce sexually by releasing eggs and sperm into the water, an event called spawning. This usually takes place during a certain time in the moon's cycle. The larvae swim for a few days before settling and secreting their own skeletons to begin a new colony.

Amazing facts

- A few corals, such as the small, solitary cup corals, can survive in the cold water off the Norwegian and Scottish coasts.
- Staghorn corals are the fastest-growing corals on a reef. They would take over the reef were it not for the fact that they are easily damaged in storms. The massive, encrusting forms, such as brain corals, are wave resistant.

Jellyfish

Jellyfish are bell-shaped animals that float in the upper layer of the ocean. They get their name from the thick layer of jelly between their ectoderms and endoderms.

Body features

The body of the jellyfish is like a bell with a mouth hanging down from the underside. Around the mouth are extensions called oral arms. Masses of tentacles hang down from the bell, each covered in thousands of sting cells. The sting cells shoot out a poisonous, harpoon-like thread whenever they are triggered by touch. In many species, the rim of the bell contains organs that sense balance and orientation. The rim also contains photoreceptors that are sensitive to light and allow the animal to know which way to move toward the surface of the water.

Jellyfish swim by contracting muscle fibers in their bells. As a jellyfish's bell contracts, water is forced out. This pushes the jellyfish along. However, this movement is too weak to help jellyfish swim against ocean currents. Normally they drift along on the ocean currents. Jellyfish often wash up on beaches after storms.

▼ Swarms of jellyfish called sea nettles occur off the coast of the eastern United States in summer. Their presence in the water prevents people from swimming.

Amazing facts

- A jellyfish's body is 96 percent water.
- Jellyfish vary in size. The diameter of the bell can range from less than 1 inch (2.5 centimeters) to more than 6 feet (2 meters). The largest jellyfish is *Cyanea arctica*, which has tentacles that reach lengths of more than 130 feet (40 meters)!
- Many jellyfish are bioluminescent, which means they can produce their own light. Some produce light to frighten away predators.

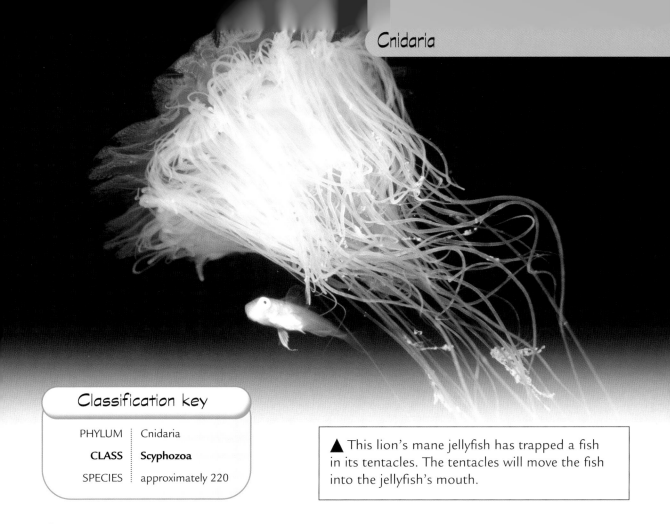

Classification key

PHYLUM	Cnidaria
CLASS	**Scyphozoa**
SPECIES	approximately 220

▲ This lion's mane jellyfish has trapped a fish in its tentacles. The tentacles will move the fish into the jellyfish's mouth.

Feeding

Jellyfish are carnivores that eat mostly plankton and young fish. First they stun their prey with their sting cells and then they use their tentacles to bring the food to their mouths. Some jellyfish swim to the surface, turn over, and then float downward with their tentacles trailing. This forms a wide net that they use to trap crustaceans and small fish.

Life cycle

Most jellyfish are thought to live for about a year. Their life cycle starts with larval jellyfish settling on the seabed. These grow into polyps that reproduce asexually by budding. Tiny medusae are pinched off the parent polyp and drift away in the water. These medusae grow into the adult jellyfish. The adults reproduce sexually by releasing gametes into the water. Fertilization takes place and the resulting larvae grow into polyps, starting the cycle again.

▲ Deep sea jellyfish have stiff tentacles. They are found at depths between 650 and 23,000 feet (200 and 7,000 meters). However, at night they feed near the surface.

Hydrozoa

The Hydrozoa class is varied. Some hydrozoans are small, but others are huge and they come in a range of colors and shapes. The Hydrozoa class is usually divided into five orders: Trachylinida, Hydroida, Milleporina, Stylasterina, and Siphonophorida.

Amazing facts

- Milleporina and Stylasterina are known as fire corals because of their coral-like growth and painful stings.
- Some medusae can rise or descend in the water by as much as 1,000 feet (300 meters) in an hour.
- Hydrozoans of the genus *Hydractinia* form a dense covering over the shells occupied by hermit crabs. They are thought to defend the crab from predators, while benefiting from scraps of food that the crab carries around.

Hydra

One of the best known hydrozoans is *Hydra,* which belongs to the order Hydroida. These tiny freshwater animals are less than an inch long and consist of a tube that ends in a ring of tentacles around the mouth. The color of each species of *Hydra* is produced by microscopic green algae living in its cells.

► There are two types of polyps on this sea fir, which belongs to the genus *Obelia*. There are feeding polyps with tentacles and reproductive polyps producing medusae.

▲ The by-the-wind sailor belongs to the order Stylasterina. It is blown across the oceans as the wind catches its upright triangular float.

Classification key

PHYLUM	Cnidaria
CLASS	**Hydrozoa**
ORDERS	Trachylinida, Hydroida, Milleporina, Stylasterina, and Siphonophorida
SPECIES	About 2,700

Animals of the *Hydra* genus use a sticky disc at the end of their bodies to attach themselves to waterweed or stones. When they want to move quickly, they somersault. They bend over and attach their tentacles to the ground and then swing their bases over their tentacles to land on the other side.

Colonies

The *Hydra* genus is unusual because it lives alone. Most of the other hydrozoans form colonies made up of thousands of polyps. Hydrocorals form large colonies that secrete a hard skeleton and resemble corals. Other hydrozoans form mats that are often mistaken for seaweed. Some of the largest hydrozoans that form colonies are confused with jellyfish.

▼ Hydrocoral is usually pink or purple and it can be found at depths of up to 66 feet (20 meters).

Medusae

Like other cnidarians, hydrozoans have a life cycle in which there are polyps and medusae. The medusa resembles a jellyfish. One feature that distinguishes it from the medusae of other species is the presence of a structure called a velum. This is a rim that projects inward around the edge of the bell, partially closing the opening. The hydrozoan medusae swim just like the jellyfish, by alternately contracting and relaxing the muscles in the bell. The advantage of a partially closed opening is that water can be pushed out with greater force, moving the animal by a kind of jet propulsion.

23

The Portuguese Man-of-war

The Portuguese man-of-war may look like a jellyfish, but it belongs to the class Hydrozoa. It is a gigantic colony of individual polyps floating on the ocean. Hanging below are several feet of tentacles covered in sting cells. The man-of-war is found in warm seas around the world, especially in tropical and subtropical regions of the Pacific and Indian oceans and in the northern Atlantic Gulf Stream.

▶ The blue, gas-filled float of the Portuguese man-of-war lies on the surface of the water where it catches the wind. Hanging below are many long tentacles.

Classification key

PHYLUM	Cnidaria
CLASS	Hydrozoa
ORDER	Siphonophora
FAMILY	Physaliidae
GENUS	*Physalia*
SPECIES	***Physalia physalis***

Catching the wind

The man-of-war's body consists of a gas-filled float called the pneumatophore. This is translucent pink, blue, or violet. The float is as much as 12 inches (30 centimeters) long and rises 6 inches (15 centimeters) or so above the water. It acts as a sail. Hanging beneath the pneumatophore are tentacles up to 164 feet (50 meters) in length. They are covered in 3 kinds of polyps: one responsible for detecting and capturing prey, one for digesting prey, and one for producing and releasing the gametes that the man-of-war needs to reproduce. The three kinds of polyps are totally dependent on each other.

Feeding

The man-of-war eats anything that comes into contact with its stinging polyps, including crustaceans and small fish. As it drifts in the ocean, its long tentacles trail through the water. Once it catches a prey animal, muscles in the tentacles contract and bring the prey close to the polyps that digest food.

Life cycle

The life cycle starts with the man-of-war reproducing sexually. The reproductive polyps release gametes into the water. Fertilization takes place when the gametes fuse and form a new individual. This grows into a larva. The larval man-of-war reproduces asexually by budding, but the buds do not separate. They remain attached, forming a colony. In time the colony develops into a full-sized man-of-war. The reproductive polyps form and sexual reproduction can take place again.

▲ The man-of-war's tentacles are covered in sting cells. Even a piece of tentacle that has broken off can give a painful sting.

Amazing facts

- The sting of the Portuguese man-of-war is painful to human beings and can have serious effects, including fever, shock, and interference with heart and lung function.

- The poison released by the sting cells is about 75 percent as powerful as cobra venom.

- Swarms, or groups, of Portuguese man-of-wars can form that number as many as several thousand.

Worms

◀ Fanworms belong to the phylum Annelida because their bodies are made up of many segments.

The group of invertebrates known as worms is split into three phyla: Platyhelminthes, or flatworms; Nematoda, or roundworms; and Annelida, segmented worms. Worms are found in both fresh and salt water, and in damp land habitats. Some worms are parasites that live on or in other animals known as hosts. A parasite feeds on the host, causing it harm.

Three cell layers

While cnidarians have two layers of cells and some of their cells are organized to form tissues, they do not have any organs. Worms, on the other hand, are more complex than the cnidarians because they have three cell layers and distinct organs. Since they have three cell layers, worms are described as triploblastic animals. There is an outer layer called the ectoderm, an inner layer called the endoderm, and a middle layer called the mesoderm.

Classification key	
PHYLA	Platyhelminthes
	Nematoda
	Annelida

The mesoderm is very important because the cells in this layer form muscles and other structures. This allows the animal to grow larger and have a firmer body. The organs are composed of various tissues that work together to carry out a particular function, such as reproduction. Some of the organs work together to form a system, such as the digestive or nervous systems.

The most primitive of the worms are the flatworms. They have a long, flat body with no circulatory system. Roundworms and the segmented worms, on the other hand, have more complex bodies. The mesoderm is split to form a large, central body cavity. In segmented worms, this cavity is filled with fluid. The fluid bathes all the internal organs and gives support to the body, forming a hydroskeleton that helps the animal to move.

Heads

While cnidarians do not have heads, worms have more developed heads. They have a definite front end that has sense organs and always ventures first into new environments, with the rear end following. The sense organs allow the animal to detect any danger ahead.

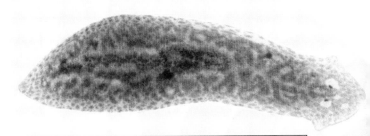

▲ This is a free-living flatworm that lives in water. It belongs to the class Turbellaria in the phylum Platyhelminthes. Other classes of flatworms live in hosts as parasites.

▼ Roundworms belong to the phylum Nematoda. Most live in the soil, but many are parasites that live in the bodies of other animals or on plants.

Flatworms

If you drop a piece of meat into a stream, within a few hours it will probably be covered in small, black worms, each about 0.4 inches (1 centimeter) long. These are flatworms called *Planaria* that live under stones in ponds and streams. *Planaria* is just one flatworm genus that belongs to the phylum Platyhelminthes. The name comes from two words: *platy* meaning "flat" and *helminthes* meaning "worms." Platyhelminthes used to be formed from three classes: Cestoda, Turbellaria, and Trematoda. More recently scientists added a fourth class: Monogenea.

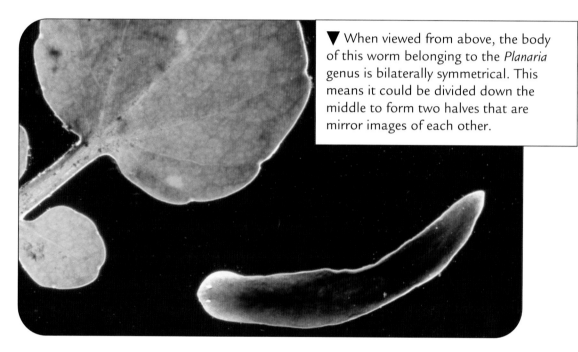

▼ When viewed from above, the body of this worm belonging to the *Planaria* genus is bilaterally symmetrical. This means it could be divided down the middle to form two halves that are mirror images of each other.

Body shape

Flatworms have long, flat bodies. Gas exchange can take place anywhere on the large surface area. The flat body means that the oxygen does not have to spread out very far to reach all of the body cells. Some flatworms have an obvious head with eyes and other sense organs. They have a mouth that leads to a stomach, but they do not have an anus at the other end of the stomach. This means that the mouth is used to take in food and expel waste. Inside, the stomach is divided into many branches so that the food reaches all parts of the body.

Classification key

PHYLUM	Platyhelminthes
CLASSES	**Cestoda, Monogenea, Trematoda, and Turbellaria**
ORDERS	35
SPECIES	approximately 13,000

▶ Liver flukes are parasites that belong to the class Trematoda. A liver fluke uses a sucker to attach itself to the body of its host.

Tapeworms belong to the class Cestoda. They are parasitic and live in the guts of vertebrates, including human beings. Turbellaria consists mostly of free-living flatworms such as the *Planaria* genus. They are covered with tiny hairs called cilia. The cilia create a current that allows the animal to glide over the river or pond bottom. Trematoda and Monogenea are made up of parasitic flukes. Flukes do not have cilia. They have a thick outer cuticle and suckers that they use to cling to their hosts. Some flukes cling to the outside of their hosts. For example, fish flukes hang onto the skin or gills of fish and feed on their blood. Other flukes invade their host's body and live in organs such as the liver.

Amazing facts

○ Worms of the *Planaria* genus have amazing powers of regeneration. If a vertical cut is made down their head end, the cells regrow to form two heads.

○ Millions of people are infected by the blood fluke that causes the disease schistosomiasis. People who stand in rice paddies planting rice plants are often infected by this fluke. The parasite burrows through the skin and enters the blood system. The infected person gradually gets weaker.

▶ This marine flatworm glides over the seabed looking for food. It feeds on small invertebrates and dead animals.

The Tapeworm

Tapeworms are very common parasites found in almost every species of vertebrate, including human beings. Their bodies are completely adapted to the life of a parasite. They do not need to move around or find food, so they have no means of moving and no sense organs. They live in the intestines of their host,s feeding on the food the hosts have digested. They do not even need a mouth. Instead, they absorb digested food through their huge surface area.

The tapeworm's body is divided into sections called proglottids. New proglottids form all the time from behind the head. The oldest are at the tail end of the tapeworm and they drop off when they are mature. Each proglottid has its own set of reproductive organs. By the time one drops off, it is full of fertilized eggs. These proglottids pass out with the host's feces.

Classification key

PHYLUM	Platyhelminthes
CLASS	Cestoda
GENUS	*Taenia*
SPECIES	***Taenia serialis***

▶ A tapeworm spends its life inside the intestines of its host. New segments are continuously formed behind the head, so the tapeworm gets longer and longer.

Amazing facts

- The largest tapeworm that lives in humans is the broad fish tapeworm, which can reach more than 60 feet (18 meters) in length. Tapeworms living in whales can reach 100 feet (30 meters) long!

- The only way to get rid of a tapeworm is to take a drug that kills the head and causes it to detach from the intestinal wall.

Life cycle

All tapeworms have a life cycle that involves two hosts. Most tapeworms are species specific, which means that the adult will grow in only one particular species. For example, it may infect dogs and not cats. One type of dog tapeworm lives in two hosts: the dog and the rabbit. The primary, or main, host is the dog. Eggs of the tapeworm pass out of the dog's intestines in its feces. Rabbits may pick up the eggs when they feed on grass. Inside the rabbit's stomach, the hard protective coat of the egg is digested and the embryo is released. Armed with six sharp hooks, the embryo burrows through the stomach wall into the blood stream. It is carried in the blood to the muscles, where it settles and grows into a bladder worm.

There is no further development until the rabbit is killed and the muscle is eaten by a dog. Inside the dog, the head of the bladder worm attaches to the wall of the intestine. Surrounded by an abundant supply of food, the tapeworm soon grows a long body and starts to produce eggs.

▲ Once the bladder worm has entered the intestine of a dog, the head of the tapeworm is released and it attaches to the wall of the intestines.

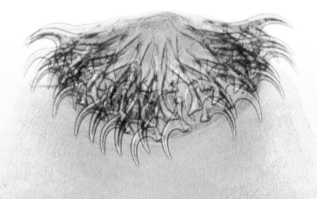

◄ The head of the dog tapeworm has hooks and suckers. These are used to attach the tapeworm firmly to the intestinal wall. This means the tapeworm is not carried out of the intestine as the food passes through.

Roundworms

Roundworms, or nematodes, are among the most abundant of all animals. They are found in almost every kind of habitat. They live in the sea, in freshwater, and in soil from the polar regions to the tropics. There are so many roundworms that a shovelful of soil probably contains millions of them.

▲ This roundworm belongs to the class Adenophorea. Soil is full of roundworms. Many roundworms are too small to be seen with the eye.

Many species

There are two classes of roundworms: Secernentea and Adenophorea. The secernentean worms are mostly parasites while the adenophoreans are mostly free-living worms. Only about 15,000 roundworm species have been described by scientists , but it has been estimated that there may be closer to 500,000 species. About 50 species have been found in human beings, 12 of which are parasitic.

▼ Roundworms are found in water, too. The pointed ends of the worm can be seen clearly.

Classification key

PHYLUM	Nematoda
CLASSES	2 (Secernentea, Adenophorea)
SPECIES	15,000 described, but likely to be more than 500,000

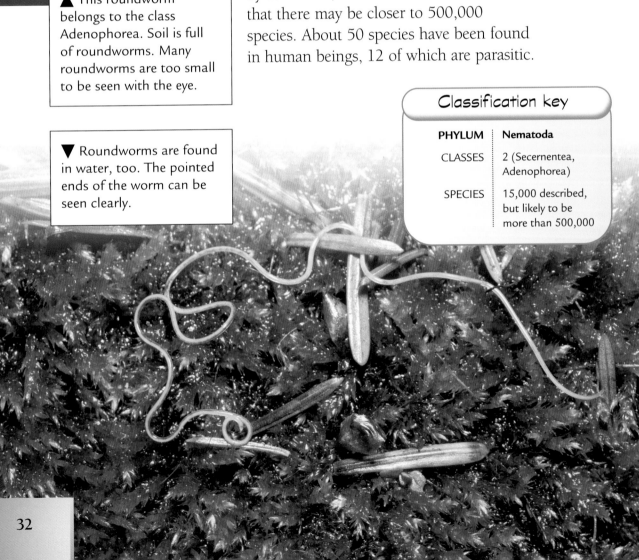

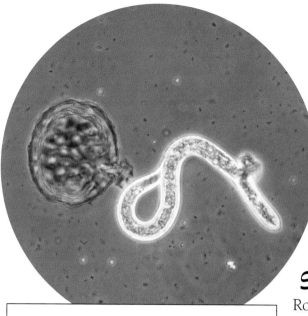

This roundworm has just hatched from its egg. The egg has a tough outer wall to protect it from being digested by the host.

Appearance

Roundworms have long, cylindrical bodies with pointed ends. The body is covered with a tough, stiff cuticle that is secreted by the ectoderm. This cuticle is replaced four times between hatching and reaching full maturity.

Sideways movement

Roundworms have an unusual sideways thrashing movement. This is because they have four blocks of muscles that run the length of the body from the head to the tail. When the muscles on one side of the body contract, the body is bent to one side. When the muscles on the other side contract, the body is bent in the opposite direction. This is a very slow and inefficient way of moving around.

Parasites

There are many parasitic roundworm species. One that is particularly important is the roundworm *Ascaris lumbricoides*, which lives in the intestine. It is thought to infect one sixth of the world's human population. Every day the worm releases hundreds of thousands of eggs that leave the body in the feces. In places where hygiene is poor, the eggs may contaminate food or water and then pass into other human beings. Once the eggs are in the stomach, the tiny worms break out and enter the bloodstream. They can block small blood vessels, especially those in the lungs. This causes fluid to collect in the lungs, resulting in a serious form of pneumonia. These worms eventually return to the intestines where they develop into adult worms.

Amazing facts

- Scientists frequently perform basic experiments with roundworms because they are inexpensive and simple. They can fit 10,000 roundworms on a single lab dish.
- One study reported around 90,000 individual roundworms in a single rotting apple.

Segmented Worms

The annelids, or segmented worms, are found around the world. Marine annelids live everywhere from shallow coastal waters to the deepest ocean sediments. Some marine annelids drift and swim across the seas, preying on plankton. On land, earthworms are found in soil, while leeches live in fresh water or in damp places such as rain forests.

▲ This giant earthworm, which lives in a rain forest, has come to the surface after a rainstorm.

Tubular body

The body of an annelid is like a tube within a tube. The outer tube is the body wall made up of the ectoderm and two layers of muscles. The inner tube is the stomach or endoderm. Between the two is the body cavity, or coelom, which is filled with fluid. This fluid provides a firm base for the muscle to push against as the worm moves around.

Annelids are far more complex than flatworms. They have a well-developed circulatory system with blood vessels and five simple hearts that pump the blood around the body. The gut has a mouth and an anus. This means that food can be continuously taken in by the mouth, processed as it passes through the body, and released as waste at the other end. Annelids also have a simple nervous system. They absorb oxygen from the air through moist skin.

▶ The spaghetti worm is a marine worm. It hides its body in a tube and sends long tentacles out to bring food to its mouth.

Segments

Annelids have bodies that are made up of many parts called segments. Each segment is separated from the neighboring segments and has its own organs to carry out respiration, excretion, and movement. The only parts of the body that do not follow this pattern are the head, which has the sense organs, and the very last segment of the body.

Chaetae

A distinctive feature of annelids is their chaetae, or bristles. Chaetae vary in shape, ranging from long, thin filaments to multipronged hooks. The two annelid classes differ in the number and size of the chaetae. The Polychaeta, as the name suggests, have many chaetae, while the earthworms in the class Clitellata have few chaetae.

Amazing facts

- The word *Annelida* comes from the Latin word *anellus*, meaning "a little ring." This refers to the ringlike segments of these worms.
- The giant earthworms of Australia can be found by the gurgling sounds they make as they tunnel underground. They can be 13 feet (4 meters) long and have up to 500 segments.
- Small worms live for only 45 to 60 days, but some large ones may live to more than 50 years of age.

Classification key

PHYLUM	Annelida
CLASSES	2 (Polychaeta, Clitellata)
SPECIES	approximately 12,000

◀ The fireworm has hollow, poison-filled bristles. They break off and then embed themselves in predators, such as fish.

Polychaetes

Polychaeta is the largest and most varied of the annelid classes and includes bristle worms, lugworms, and fanworms. The Latin word *polychaetae* means "many chaetae," or bristles. Some of the polychaetes are free-living, but many live in burrows or tubes.

Amazing facts

- The fireworms have chaetae made of calcium carbonate or silica. These chaetae are brittle and contain poisons. When the chaetae penetrate the skin of a predator, they break and cause a burning sensation.
- The palolo worm lives in coral reefs. To reproduce, it grows a tail section packed with either sperm or eggs. Five days after the first full moon in October, the tail sections of all the palolo worms break free and wiggle to the surface of the water. There, the released eggs are fertilized by the sperm.

▼ The bobbit worm often lies in the sediment on the seabed. It pounces on small fish swimming above it, pulling the fish under the sediment to be eaten.

Features

One characteristic feature of Polychaetes is a structure called a parapodium. The word means "side foot" and it is a flap that sticks out of the side of each segment and has chaetae growing from it. Polychaetes have well-developed heads with between two and four pairs of eyes, a number of sensory "feelers" and a brain. Many have powerful jaws and long tentacles that collect food. Most have a well-developed blood circulation.

Classification key

PHYLUM	Annelida
CLASS	**Polychaeta**
ORDERS	22
SPECIES	9,000

▼ This ragworm swims using its parapodia as paddles to push through the water.

▼ Most fireworms are scavengers. This fireworm is searching for food in the open shell of a dead clam.

Lifestyle

Polychaetes can be divided into two types: those that are free-living and those that live sedentary lives. The free-living polychaetes have well-developed parapodia with chaetae that they use to swim. The most active species need plenty of oxygen, so some of their parapodia are modified to form gills. The free-swimming worms are usually carnivorous and they can chase after prey such as other worms and small invertebrates.

The sedentary worms spend much of their time in burrows in the mud or sand, or in tubes they have built. Examples of sedentary worms include lugworms, parchment worms, and fanworms.

Reproduction

A few polychaetes can reproduce asexually by budding or dividing their bodies into separate parts. However, most polychaetes reproduce sexually. Polychaete worms are either male or female. The worms gather together and release eggs and sperm into the water at the same time. The eggs are fertilized and develop into free-swimming larvae that drift with the plankton before developing into adult polychaetes.

Fanworms

Fanworms are polychaetes that secrete a tube around the body. They vary in size from just a few inches to several feet in length. The fan of tentacles that emerges from the tube is often brightly colored. Fanworms are found in coastal waters, on coral reefs, and thousands of feet deep on the ocean floor.

Tubes

A fanworm builds its tube by producing a leathery mucus from a collar-like structure at the base of its tentacles. Particles of sand and mud collected in the tentacles are incorporated into the tube. Some tubes are very long and stick out above the seabed. Others are buried in the mud or sand and are difficult to see. These worms are extremely sensitive to shadows and vibrations. If the worms are disturbed, they quickly pull back into their tube and close a kind of door over the top.

▲ The fanworm feeds by extending its tentacles into the water. The tentacles trap food drifting in the water.

▼ The fanworm constructs its tube from sand and mud that is glued together with mucus.

The worm extends a fan of tentacles from the top of the tube to feed. The tentacles extract both oxygen and food from the water. Small particles of food are flicked toward the mouth by tiny cilia. Larger particles are mixed with mucus to lengthen the tube. Living on the seabed, the worm feeds on the food that sinks down from above.

Amazing facts

- The European fanworm attaches itself to the hulls of ships and has survived long journeys to Australia. It has become a major marine pest along the western Australian coastline.
- Sometimes people find large numbers of empty tubes of the bamboo worm washed up on beaches after a storm. The worms have not been killed. They have retreated inside their tubes and only the empty top part has broken off.

Christmas tree worm

One of the most attractive fanworms is the Christmas tree worm. Christmas tree worms spawn in October at low tide. The eggs are fertilized and grow into larvae that settle on coral. Once settled on the coral, it starts to secrete its tube.

▼ The Christmas tree worm gets its name from its brightly colored, spiraling tentacles.

Classification key

PHYLUM	Annelida
CLASS	Polychaeta
SUBCLASS	Sedentaria
FAMILY	**Sabellidae**
SPECIES	approximately 9,000

Clitellates

The clitellates are annelids that have a swelling behind the head called a clitellum. These worms have bodies with few or no chaetae. The class is divided into two subclasses: Hirudinea (leeches) and Oligochaeta (earthworms).

Earthworms

Earthworms are burrowing worms that live in soil. At night an earthworm extends the front half of its body from its burrow in search of food such as leaves and seeds. The hind end stays firmly in the burrow. Worms spend most of their time eating leaves or soil. The food passes through the stomach, where the valuable nutrients are digested. The rest passes out and is deposited in a pile by the entrance to the burrow. These piles are called worm castings.

Classification key

PHYLUM	Annelida
CLASS	**Clitellata**
SUBCLASSES	2 (Oligochaeta, Hirudinea)
SPECIES	approximately 3,000

Amazing facts

- It is incredibly difficult to pull an earthworm from its burrow because it pushes its chaetae into the soil that forms the burrow walls.
- Earthworms have a giant nerve fiber that runs the length of the body. This allows nerve impulses to travel quickly and is essential for the worm's escape response. If a worm is touched by a bird or other predator, it will suddenly contract its whole body and disappear into its burrow.

▲ The front end of the earthworm is more pointed than the hind end. Here the head of an earthworm emerges from its burrow.

▼ An earthworm is pulling a leaf into its burrow. There may be between 50 and 500 earthworms in every square yard of soil. Their castings make the soil richer.

Moving

Earthworms have a simple nervous system that coordinates muscle contraction during movement. The worm uses its two sets of muscles to move. When the circular muscles contract, each segment becomes long and thin. When the longitudinal muscles that stretch along the length of the worm contract, the worm becomes short and fat. First the worm extends the front of its body by contracting the circular muscles in these segments. It sticks out its chaetae to grip the soil. Then it pulls the back end of its body forward by contracting its longitudinal muscles. By alternating these two muscle sets, the worm can move forward.

Reproduction

Earthworms have both male and female sex organs, so they are called hermaphrodites. However, whenever they meet another worm they exchange sperm. During egg laying, the clitellum secretes a ring of mucus that glides forward over the body of the worm. As it moves, it picks up both eggs and sperm, and fertilization takes place in the mucus. Then the ring slips off the worm and lies in the soil. It hardens to form a cocoon in which the eggs develop and from which the young worms finally escape.

▼ This pair of earthworms are exchanging sperm. The head of one worm lies next to the hind end of the other worm.

Leeches

Leeches are found in a wide variety of habitats, but they are more common in shallow, slow-flowing streams, lakes, and ponds. They are numerous in nutrient-rich water, such as in lakes and ponds polluted with farm waste and sewage. Leeches are also found in tropical rain forests. Many people think all leeches are bloodsuckers. However, although there are many bloodsucking species, some leeches scavenge on dead and decaying matter.

▲ Leeches, such as this medicinal leech, have a small sucker beside the mouth and a larger one at the rear end that they use to attach to host animals.

▼ A tiger leech waits for a host animal to pass close by. It will drop the instant it senses an animal passing below.

Features

Leeches have between 32 and 34 segments, regardless of their size. Once this number is reached, they do not grow any more. In other annelids, the number of segments increases with age. Strangely, the rings on the outside of a leech do not correspond to the segments inside the body. Leeches do not have any chaetae, so the outsides of their bodies are smooth.

Amazing facts

- The giant Amazonian leech, *Haementeria ghiliani*, reaches just over 12 inches (30 centimeters) in length.

- Some leeches can survive periods of drought by burrowing into the mud at the bottom of lakes and ponds. They can tolerate the loss of 90 percent of their body weight.

- The saliva of the medicinal leech contains substances that act as powerful antibiotics and anesthetics, or painkillers. These could be very useful in treating patients in the future.

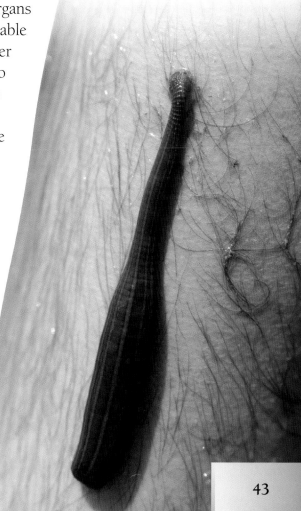

▼ The saliva of the leech contains a substance called hirudin that prevents the host's blood from clotting while the leech is feeding.

Blood suckers

Most leeches are semiparasitic, and they feed on the blood of vertebrates. Unlike parasitic flatworms, they have to move to find a host, so they have sense organs and they can swim. Once a leech has found a suitable host, it attaches itself to the outside using the larger rear sucker. It uses small jaws around its mouth to make a small wound. The leech drops off once its gut is swollen with blood, and then it digests its huge meal. Leeches do not feed often, so they take in enough blood to last for several months.

Medicinal leeches

The medicinal leech, as its name suggests, was used in the past for medicinal purposes—mainly to remove what was thought to be bad blood from diseased patients. Today, the medicinal leech is making a comeback. It is used to relieve the buildup of pressure and to restore blood circulation in patients who have had severed body parts, such as fingers and ears, reattached. Leeches can also stop scabs from sealing over a wound too quickly.

Echinoderms

Echinoderms are spiny-skinned animals such as sea stars, sea urchins, and sea cucumbers. They are marine animals found around the world, on rocky and sandy shores, in estuaries, on coral reefs, and on the seabed.

Spiny skeleton

The three most common characteristics of echinoderms are a symmetrical body that is usually divided into five parts, tube feet, and a skeleton. The skeleton lies just underneath the skin. It is formed from plates of calcium carbonate. The plates remain separate in sea stars and brittle stars, but are fitted together to form a more rigid ball shape in sea urchins. Spiny extensions and knobs stick out from the body.

▲ Echinoderms, such as this sea star, have no head or tail but they do have mouths. The mouth of the sea star is on its lower surface.

Water vascular system

Echinoderms have an unusual system of water-filled tubes or canals that run through their bodies. Water is sucked into the system through a perforated plate called the madreporite that usually lies on the surface of the body. A canal leads from the madreporite to a circular canal around the mouth. Further canals lead off this circular canal down each of the arms of the animal. The canals end in rows of tentacles called tube feet.

▲ Sea urchins are spherical in shape. Their bodies are completely encased in spiny skeletons.

Regrowing body parts

Some echinoderms have excellent powers of regeneration. If disturbed, brittle stars can shed an arm or part of an arm. This allows them to escape while the cast-off arm continues to wriggle, distracting the attacker. It was this behavior that gave them their name. However, regeneration is only possible as long as part of the arm remains attached to the central disc. Sea stars can also regrow arms bitten off by predators.

▲ Brittle stars belong to the class Ophuroidea. Each has a small body with five long arms.

Five classes

The phylum Echinodermata is formed of two subphyla: Pelmatozoa and Eleutherozoa. The subphylum Pelmatozoa contains one class: Crinoidea. This is an ancient group that contains sea lilies and feather stars. Eleutherozoa is divided into four classes: Asteroidea includes sea stars or sea stars; Ophuroidea includes brittle stars and basket stars; Echinoidea includes sea urchins; and Holothuroidea includes sea cucumbers.

Amazing facts

- The word *echinodermata* is Greek for "spiny skin."
- The regeneration of an arm may take as long as a year to complete.
- The spines of many sea urchin species are very thin and brittle. They are sometimes are coated in a poisonous substance or have a poison gland attached.

Classification key

PHYLUM	Echinodermata
SUBPHYLA	2 (Pelmatozoa, Eleutherozoa)
CLASSES	5 (Crinoidea, Asteroidea, Ophuroidea, Echinoidea, Holothuroidea)
SPECIES	approximately 6,000

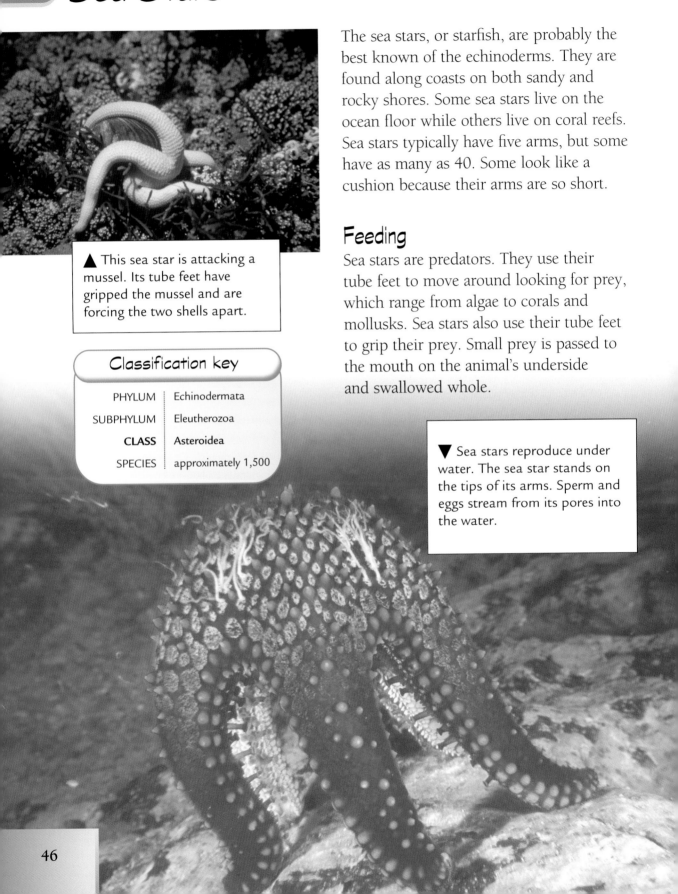

Sea Stars

The sea stars, or starfish, are probably the best known of the echinoderms. They are found along coasts on both sandy and rocky shores. Some sea stars live on the ocean floor while others live on coral reefs. Sea stars typically have five arms, but some have as many as 40. Some look like a cushion because their arms are so short.

Feeding

Sea stars are predators. They use their tube feet to move around looking for prey, which range from algae to corals and mollusks. Sea stars also use their tube feet to grip their prey. Small prey is passed to the mouth on the animal's underside and swallowed whole.

▲ This sea star is attacking a mussel. Its tube feet have gripped the mussel and are forcing the two shells apart.

Classification key

PHYLUM	Echinodermata
SUBPHYLUM	Eleutherozoa
CLASS	Asteroidea
SPECIES	approximately 1,500

▼ Sea stars reproduce under water. The sea star stands on the tips of its arms. Sperm and eggs stream from its pores into the water.

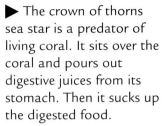
▶ The crown of thorns sea star is a predator of living coral. It sits over the coral and pours out digestive juices from its stomach. Then it sucks up the digested food.

The sea star uses its tube feet to pry open the shells of bivalves such as clams and mussels. It wraps its arms around the two shells of the bivalve and begins the slow process of forcing them apart. Once there is a tiny gap, the sea star turns out its stomach through its mouth and inserts the stomach through the narrow gap into the bivalve. The stomach secretes digestive enzymes to break down the bivalve's body into a liquid that is absorbed by the lining of the stomach. A sea star can take eight hours to digest a large mussel.

Amazing facts

- A single female crown of thorns sea star can produce up to 100 million eggs per year.
- A tiny crab called *Trapezia cymodoce* protects the coral *Pocillopora damicornis* from being preyed upon by the crown of thorns sea star by breaking off its spines.
- Sea stars and other echinoderms have tiny pincers on the surface of their skin called pedicellaria. These pincers catch any small animal that walks over the surface of the sea star. They also help to keep the surface free of debris.

Reproduction

Many sea stars undergo asexual reproduction when parts of their bodies break off and regenerate. Sometimes the leg of a sea star will simply walk away from the rest of the body. Sexual reproduction involves the release of gametes into the water. In some species, there is a mass spawning when the water reaches a certain temperature. All the sea stars in the area release their eggs and sperm at the same time, increasing the chances of fertilization.

Sea Lilies and Feather Stars

The sea lilies and feather stars belong to the class Crinoidea, an ancient class with many fossil examples. Sea lilies are found in deep water while feather stars are found mostly on coral reefs.

Sea lilies

Sea lilies can be found at depths of 330 feet (100 meters) or more. They are made up of three parts. The animal is attached to the seabed by its central stalk. The middle part of the individual is called the cup or calyx. Attached to the cup are five long arms. Sea lilies remain attached to the central stalk throughout their lives. The stalk lifts the crown of arms above the seabed so that it is more likely to catch small animals.

Feather Stars

Feather stars have five long arms, and they resemble sea lilies. However, feather stars break away from their stalks when they are young. Instead of stalks, feather stars have a cluster of curling, rootlike structures to attach themselves to coral or rock. Some feather stars can swim considerable distances.

Amazing facts

- One extinct crinoid, *Extracrinus subangularis*, had a stalk more than 70 feet (21 meters) long.
- In places on the Great Barrier Reef, feather stars swarm in large numbers, covering the floor of tidal pools with great brown masses of writhing bodies.

◀ The five arms of a feather star are divided many times. The feather star extends these arms to feed.

▲ The arms of a feather star look like bird feathers and give the animal its name.

Filter feeders

Both feather stars and sea lilies are filter feeders that use their arms to catch food. Feather stars are nocturnal, extending their arms only at night to feed on plankton. They do not move around very much, but find a position on the reef where currents bring a constant supply of small animals. Often they are found sitting on fan corals because these corals grow in places where there is a current. Once in position, they stretch out their arms to form a fan. Each arm has a double row of tube feet that line a sticky groove that runs down the arm to the mouth. The mouth is on top of the calyx. When a piece of food touches an arm, a tube foot grabs it. Then it is moved along the sticky food grooves into the mouth.

Classification key

PHYLUM	Echinodermata
SUBPHYLUM	Pelmatozoa
CLASS	**Crinoidea**
SPECIES	approximately 630

Reproduction

Sea lilies and feather stars can regenerate lost arms. The adult animals are of separate sexes and they undergo sexual reproduction. The eggs and sperm are released into the water. Fertilized eggs develop into free-swimming larvae that settle on the seabed and develop into miniature sea lilies and feather stars.

Sea Urchins

Sea urchins look very different from sea stars. They have a spherical, or ball-shaped, body that is covered in spines. Most sea urchins are between 2 and 5 inches (6 and 12 centimeters) in diameter, but some are as large as 14 inches (35 centimeters) in diameter. Sea urchins are found in a variety of marine habitats. Some live among the rocks of rocky shores and on coral reefs. Others are found buried in the sand of beaches and estuaries.

A ball of spines

Sea urchins do not have arms. They are either spherical or flattened in shape. The skeleton is made up of five closely fitting plates that form a rounded shell completely enclosing the soft parts. Numerous spines stick out from the shell. The spines are joined to the skeleton by a ball-and-socket joint, like that of the human hip or shoulder. This means the spine can move in the joint. Sea urchins use their spines to wedge themselves into holes and crevices.

Classification key	
PHYLUM	Echinodermata
SUBPHYLUM	Eleutherozoa
CLASS	**Echinoidea**
SPECIES	just under 1,000

► The sea urchin moves by extending its tube feet. The tube feet grip the seabed and pull the animal forward.

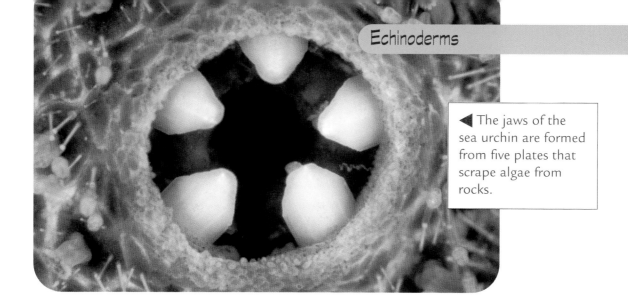

◀ The jaws of the sea urchin are formed from five plates that scrape algae from rocks.

Rows of tube feet

There are five rows of long tube feet, hidden among the spines, that the sea urchin uses to help it to move. It extends its tube feet beyond the spines. The suckers on the tube feet grip the surface and pull the animal along.

Feeding

Sea urchins hide in crevices during the day and emerge at night to feed. They creep slowly over rocks looking for algae and small animals. The mouth is on the underside. Surrounding the mouth are five jaw plates that act as powerful scraping tools.

The burrowing species feed in a different way. They feed on particles of food that they find in the mud and sand in which they are buried. Their tube feet pass the food particles to the mouth. The sea potato has long tube feet on its upper side that it uses to dig a tunnel up to the surface in order to reach the water.

Amazing facts

- Sea urchins of the *Diadema* genus have long, thin, brittle spines that break easily. The spines are covered in a poison that causes severe irritation. People often step on these urchins and get spines embedded in their feet.

- Despite their protective spines, sea urchins are eaten by other animals, such as octopus and triggerfish. The triggerfish bites off the spines so that it can crack open the body of the urchin.

- Young sand dollars swallow heavy sand grains to weigh themselves down so they are not carried away by the tides.

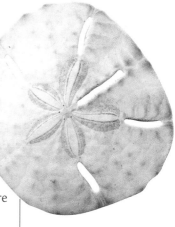

▶ Sea urchins, such as the sand dollar, have an exoskeleton formed from five plates that are fused together.

51

Brittle Stars and Sea Cucumbers

Brittle stars look like slender sea stars with long arms and a tiny central disc. They belong to the class Ophuroidea. The sea cucumber looks nothing like a sea star. It is a sausage-shaped animal with a leathery skin. It belongs to the class Holothuroidea.

▲ The arms of brittle stars are edged with rows of small spines that help the animals to feed and to fend off predators.

Brittle Stars

Brittle stars are found in large numbers on the seabed. They have five long, snakelike, feathery arms that they use to move over the seabed and to swim. Brittle stars do not rely on tube feet for movement and are the fastest moving of the echinoderms. Most brittle stars are scavengers that feed on dead animals on the seabed. Others are filter feeders that trap drifting particles of food in mucus that stretches between their arms.

Classification key

PHYLUM	Echinodermata
SUBPHYLUM	Eleutherozoa
CLASS	**Ophuroidea**
SPECIES	2,000

▼ The sea cucumber has a mass of tube feet around its mouth. These are covered in mucus to trap food and mud.

Sea cucumbers

Sea cucumbers live in sandy and muddy areas. Their mouths are surrounded by a mass of modified tube feet that form feeding tentacles. Most sea cucumbers feed on dead plant and animal material in the sand. Sea cucumbers have an unusual method of breathing. They take in water through their anus. Once the water is inside their bodies, oxygen is removed and the water is pumped out.

The pearl fish is a small fish that uses the body of the sea cucumber as a hiding place during the day. When the sea cucumber breathes, its anus opens and the fish swims inside. At night the fish emerges to feed on small fishes and shrimp.

Reproduction

Sea cucumbers undergo a mass spawning. Many sea cucumbers gather together on the seabed and, with their heads raised like snakes, they sway in the water as eggs and sperm are released from a pore on each cucumber's head. By spawning at the same time, there is a greater chance that their eggs will be fertilized.

Amazing facts

- Some sea cucumbers release poisons. Because the poison cannot disperse, sea cucumbers kept in an aquarium have been known to kill all the other animals and themselves.

- Some species of sea cucumbers release sticky, white tubes through their anus to entangle a predator. These tubes are part of their respiratory system. Some predators, such as small crabs, may become so trapped in the tubes that they are unable to free themselves and die.

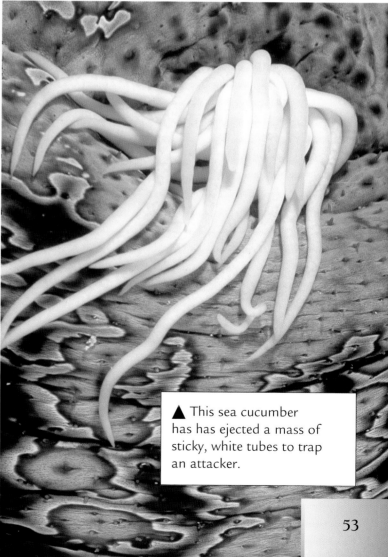

▲ This sea cucumber has has ejected a mass of sticky, white tubes to trap an attacker.

Classification key

PHYLUM	Echinodermata
SUBPHYLUM	Eleutherozoa
CLASS	**Holothuroidea**
SPECIES	1150

Disappearing Coral Reefs

Coral reefs, which are made from animals themselves, are important habitats for other marine animals. Reefs are often called the rain forests of the sea because of the great numbers of different animals and plants that live on them. Unfortunately, corals are very sensitive to slight variations in water conditions and are easily damaged by pollution or environmental changes.

Changing climates

A variety of conditions can affect corals. These include an increase in the surface temperature of the water, a decrease in sea level, or an increase in the salinity of the water resulting from a lack of rainfall. When corals are stressed by environmental changes, they lose their zooxanthellae. This means that they cannot produce enough food. They also lose their color and become white. This is called bleaching. Sometimes the corals can recover and their zooxanthellae return, but often they die. Corals under stress also suffer from more diseases. When the corals die, the animals that depend on the corals are affected, too. One of the greatest threats comes from global warming. Global warming is causing the oceans to get warmer and weather patterns to change.

◄ This coral has undergone bleaching. The algae living in it have left because of a change in the environmental conditions.

Other threats

Global warming is not the only threat to coral reefs. Pollution from sewage adds nutrients to the water, and this causes green algae to grow. The algae grow quickly and can completely cover a reef, preventing light from reaching the corals.

Sometimes a reef is blown up using dynamite. The broken coral is collected and used as a building material.

Amazing cold water coral reefs lie off the coasts of Scotland, Ireland, and Norway. These reefs are threatened by fishing because nets are dragged over them to catch fish.

▲ It is very tempting for divers to touch or even break off the corals. However, the slightest touch can damage these living organisms.

Amazing facts

- Ten percent of the world's reefs have already been damaged by human activity such as dynamiting for building materials. At current rates of destruction, 70 percent of the world's reefs may be damaged during the next few decades.

- Since the early 1980s, people have destroyed more than 35 million acres of coral reefs.

◀ In some places coral reefs are blown up with dynamite. The coral is sold as souvenirs and the rubble is used to build new tourist resorts.

Protecting Corals

Scientists are studying coral reefs to better understand them and to be able to conserve them more effectively. Many reefs are monitored using the Coral Reef Early Warning System. This system consists of buoys placed on reefs that measure air temperature, wind speed and direction, atmospheric pressure, sea temperature, salinity (levels of salt in the water), and tidal level. Every hour, this data is transmitted to scientists to describe conditions that may cause bleaching on coral reefs.

Amazing facts

- Dry Tortugas National Park in southern Florida was established in 1908 as the world's first marine protected area.
- It is estimated that coral reefs may be home to more than two million plant and animal species.
- Fishing from coral reefs provides food for nearly a billion people each year.

Coral reef protection

Coral reefs can be saved by making them protected areas. The many reefs of the Great Barrier Reef have been given different levels of protection. Leisure activities, such as snorkeling and diving, are allowed on some of the reefs, while fishing is allowed on others. Some of the most important reefs have the highest level of protection and cannot be visited at all by people.

▼ Scientists have found that shipwrecks are quickly colonized by corals that establish new reefs.

▲ Artificial reefs can be formed by sinking old trucks and ships in areas of ocean where the conditions are right for corals.

Less silt

Mangrove swamps are smelly, muddy habitats found along low-lying tropical coasts. The mass of tangled mangrove roots traps silt and prevents it from reaching and damaging coral reefs. However, many mangrove swamps have been cleared to make space for new tourist resorts and marinas. In many parts of the world, these swamps are now being replanted to protect coral reefs from the damaging silt.

Looking after the reef

Local communities around the world are realizing that their coral reefs are important. For many people living on small tropical islands, such as the Maldives, fish is a main source of protein. Coral reefs are home to many fish. Protecting coral reefs ensures that the islanders will have fish in the future. Coral reefs are natural barriers that protect islands and coasts from storms. When reefs are destroyed, that protection is lost. Also, a healthy coral reef may help the local community earn money by attracting tourists.

▶ Coral reefs may contain many coral species and support thousands of other species. This makes them one of the most diverse habitats on Earth.

Classification

Scientists know of about two million different kinds of animals. With so many species, it is important that they be classified into groups so that they can be described more accurately. The groups show how living organisms are related through evolution and where they belong in the natural world. A scientist identifies an animal by looking at features such as the number of legs or the type of teeth. Animals that share the same characteristics belong to the same species. Scientists place species with similar characteristics in the same genus. The genera are grouped together in families, which in turn are grouped into orders, and orders are grouped into classes. Classes are grouped together in phyla and finally, phyla are grouped into kingdoms. Kingdoms are the largest groups. There are five kingdoms: monerans (bacteria), protists (single-celled organisms), fungi, plants, and animals.

Naming an animal

Each species has a unique Latin name that consists of two words. The first word is the name of the genus to which the organism belongs. The second is the name of its species. For example, the Latin name of the common earthworm is *Lumbricus terrestris,* and that of the red marsh worm is *Lumbricus rubellus.* This tells us that these animals are grouped in the same genus but are different species. Latin names are used to avoid confusion. For example, in many parts of the world, echinoderms belonging to the class Asteroidea are called sea stars. However, in the United Kingdom, they are called starfish. Sometimes there are very small differences between individuals in the same species, so there is an extra division called a subspecies. To show that an animal belongs to a subspecies, another name is added to the end of the Latin name.

◀ The sea star is classified as an echinoderm because it has a spiny skin and tube feet.

This table shows how a common sea star is classified.

Classification	Example: common sea star	Features
Kingdom	Animalia	Sea stars belong to the kingdom Animalia because sea stars have many cells, need to eat food, and are formed from a fertilized egg.
Phylum	Echinodermata	An animal from the phylum Echinodermata has a spiny skin and a body based on five parts with tube feet.
Class	Asteroidea	All members of the Asteroidea have a circular body with five or more arms. The madreporite is found on the upper surface.
Order	Forcipulatida	These members have a sucker at the end of each tube foot and tiny pincers.
Family	Asteriidae	All members of this family possess four rows of tube feet.
Genus	*Asterias*	A genus is a group of species that are more closely related to one another than to any other species in the family. *Asterias* refers to the genus.
Species	*rubens*	A species is a grouping of individuals that interbreed successfully. The species name of the common sea star is *Asterias rubens*.

Invertebrate Evolution

Life first appeared on Earth about 3.8 billion years ago. These were the bacteria and other single-celled organisms. Some of these single-celled organisms evolved into simple animals. The next major step forward came when cells grouped together to form an animal with many cells. This animal was probably a sponge, and it happened about 1 billion years ago.

Most of our knowledge of the past is based on fossils, the hard remains of animals that are preserved in rocks. Unfortunately, the soft-bodied cnidarians and flatworms do not leave fossils. However, some scientists have found flowerlike patterns on the surfaces of rocks, and they believe they are the marks left by jellyfish washed up on a beach. These marks date back 650 million years.

▲ This is the fossil of a sea urchin. Sea urchins, sea stars, and sea cucumbers appeared about 250 to 200 million years ago.

One of the most important periods in the history of the natural world is the Cambrian Period, about 540 million years ago, when life was evolving at a very fast rate. Before this time there were just sponges, cnidarians, and flatworms. By the end of the Cambrian Period, all of the main groups of animals had appeared. One such group was the annelid worms. These burrowing worms helped to break down dead and decaying material, and this process released carbon dioxide gas into the atmosphere. This gas was in short supply at the time and plants needed it to carry out photosynthesis. The arrival of the annelids meant there was more carbon dioxide for the plants.

◄ Corals leave behind a limestone skeleton. They can be traced back to 600 million years ago.

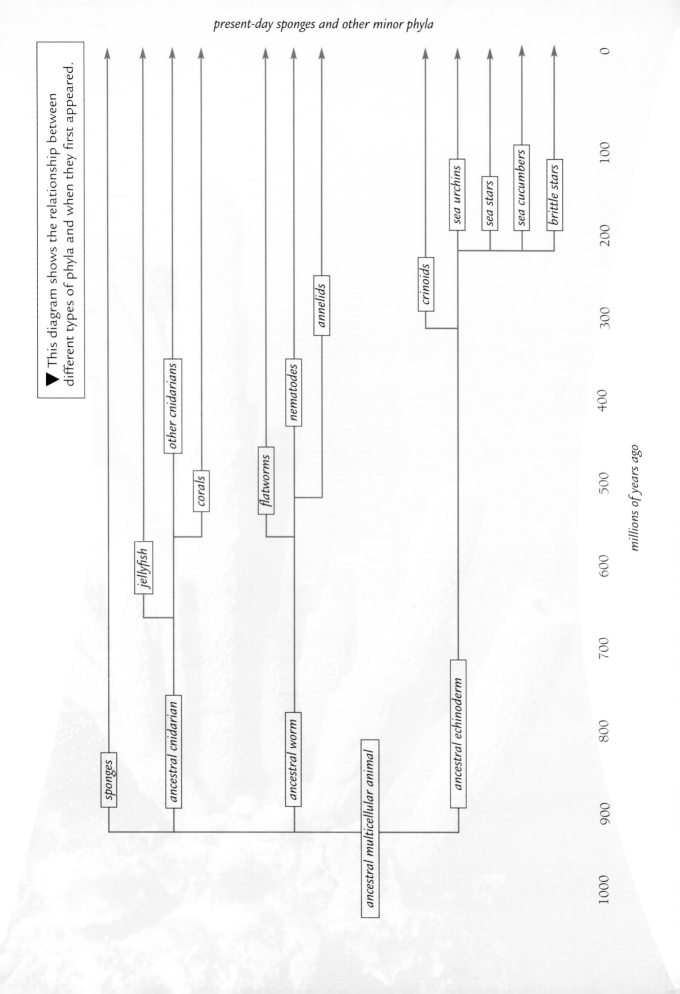

present-day sponges and other minor phyla

▶ This diagram shows the relationship between different types of phyla and when they first appeared.

sponges

jellyfish

other cnidarians

corals

ancestral cnidarian

flatworms

nematodes

annelids

ancestral worm

crinoids

sea urchins

sea stars

sea cucumbers

brittle stars

ancestral echinoderm

ancestral multicellular animal

millions of years ago

0   100   200   300   400   500   600   700   800   900   1000

Glossary

adapt change in order to cope with the environment

anemone type of marine cnidarian with a ring of tentacles around its mouth that belongs to the class Anthozoa

asexual reproduction reproduction in which one organism produces offspring that are genetically identical to the parent

bilateral on two sides

bleaching the turning white of corals following the loss of their zooxanthellae

carnivore meat eater

chaeta tiny bristle

characteristic feature or quality of an animal, such as having tentacles or bristles

cilium (plural: **cilia**) tiny hairs that beat or move

colony group of individuals living as one

crustacean arthropod, such as a crab, that has antennae, eyes on stalks, and a shieldlike covering over the head and thorax

cuticle protective outer covering found on some invertebrate animals, such as tapeworms

diploblastic having two layers of cells, called the ectoderm and endoderm

evolution slow process of change in living organisms so they can adapt to their environment

evolve change very slowly over a long period of time

excretion removal of waste products from the body

exoskeleton skeleton made of a tough material on the outside of an animal's body

extinct no longer in existence, to have permanently disappeared

feces waste produced by the body

fertilize create a cell capable of becoming a new individual through the fusing of male and female sex cells (sperm and eggs)

flagellum (plural: **flagella**) long hair or threadlike structure that is attached to a cell

fossil preserved remains of an organism

gamete sex cell, such as an egg or sperm

host organism on which a parasite lives and feeds

hermaphrodite having both male and female reproductive organs

interbreed mate with another animal of the same species

intertidal zone area of shore between the lowest low tide and the highest high tide

invertebrate animal without a backbone

larva young animal that looks different from the adult and changes appearance as it develops

medusa (plural: **medusae**) free-swimming stage in the life cycle of a cnidarian. It looks like a jellyfish.

mucus slimy substance produced by an animal's body

nervous system network of nerve cells that carry nerve impulses between parts of the body

organism living thing

osculum large pore in a sponge through which water leaves

parapodium (plural: **parapodia**) flap that sticks out from the side of a segment of a polychaete worm, often bearing chaetae

parasite organism, such as a tapeworm, that lives on or in another organism (called the host) and causes that organism harm

photosynthesis process by which plants make their own food using sunlight, carbon dioxide, and water

plankton group of small plants and animals that drift in great numbers in the upper levels of fresh or salt water

polyp sedentary stage in the life cycle of a cnidarian

predator animal that hunts other animals

prey animal that is hunted by other animals

radial symmetry divided into many equal parts arranged around a central axis

reef colony, or large group, of hard corals

regeneration regrowth

reproduce produce new organisms that are like the parent

respiration process that takes place in cells to release energy from food substances

scavenger animal that feeds on the dead bodies of other animals

sedentary remaining in one place, hardly moving

sessile attached to the seabed and unable to move from one place to another

sexual reproduction reproduction involving the production of gametes (eggs and sperm) by two parents and the fusion of an egg and sperm to form a new individual

silt small pieces of soil, rock, and other debris carried in water

skeleton framework of an animal that supports its body

spawn release eggs

species group of individuals that share many characteristics and can produce offspring

spicule small, sharp, pointed structure found in sponges and soft corals

sucker cup-shaped structure that sticks to a rock or another animal, using suction

symmetrical divided into parts of equal shape and size

tentacle part of the body that is long and trailing, as in jellyfish, or can be extended, as in anemones, in order to catch prey

territory area in which an animal or group of animals live

triploblastic having three cell layers: an ectoderm, mesoderm, and endoderm

tropics hot, often wet, region of the world between the tropic of Cancer and the tropic of Capricorn

tropical relating to the hot regions of the world that lie on either side of the equator

vertebrate animal with a backbone

zooxanthella (plural: **zooxanthellae**) alga that lives in corals, providing them with food

Further Information

Cerullo, Mary M. *Coral Reef: A City That Never Sleeps.* New York: Penguin Group, 2001.

Fullick, Ann. *Ecosystems & Environment.* Chicago: Heinemann Library, 2000.

Garcia, Eulalia et al. *Sponges: Filters of the Sea.* Milwaukee: Gareth Stevens, 1997.

Sachidhanandam, Uma. *Threatened Habitats.* Chicago: Raintree, 2004.

Telford, Carole and Rod Theodorou. *Inside a Coral Reef.* Chicago: Heinemann Library, 1998.

Index